THE FLAG'S WHISPER

A JOURNEY THROUGH TIME

SWETA SANAPALA

OrangeBooks Publication

www.orangebooks.in

OrangeBooks Publication

1st Floor, Rajhans Arcade, Mall Road, Kohka, Bhilai, Chhattisgarh 490020

Website: **www.orangebooks.in**

First Edition, 2025

ISBN: 978-93-7426-904-6

Price: Rs. 299.00

Printed in India

"Sometimes, all it takes is a whisper to awaken a nation's soul."

"To the little hearts who carry big dreams for our nation."

Acknowledgements

To my son Dhruva,
whose innocent curiosity gave this story its wings.

To the children across India,
who believe in a better tomorrow—may you always stand tall and proud.

And to you,
the reader, for choosing to listen to the flag's whisper.

It was a bright morning near the Charminar, one of the oldest and most beautiful landmarks in Hyderabad. People from all over the city gathered to celebrate Independence Day.

The sky was filled with tricolor balloons and vibrant confetti. The Indian flag soared high above the crowd, fluttering proudly in the breeze.

Among the cheering crowd stood five friends—Dhruva, Shaurya, Parnika, Guhita, and Vihaan—their faces glowing with excitement.

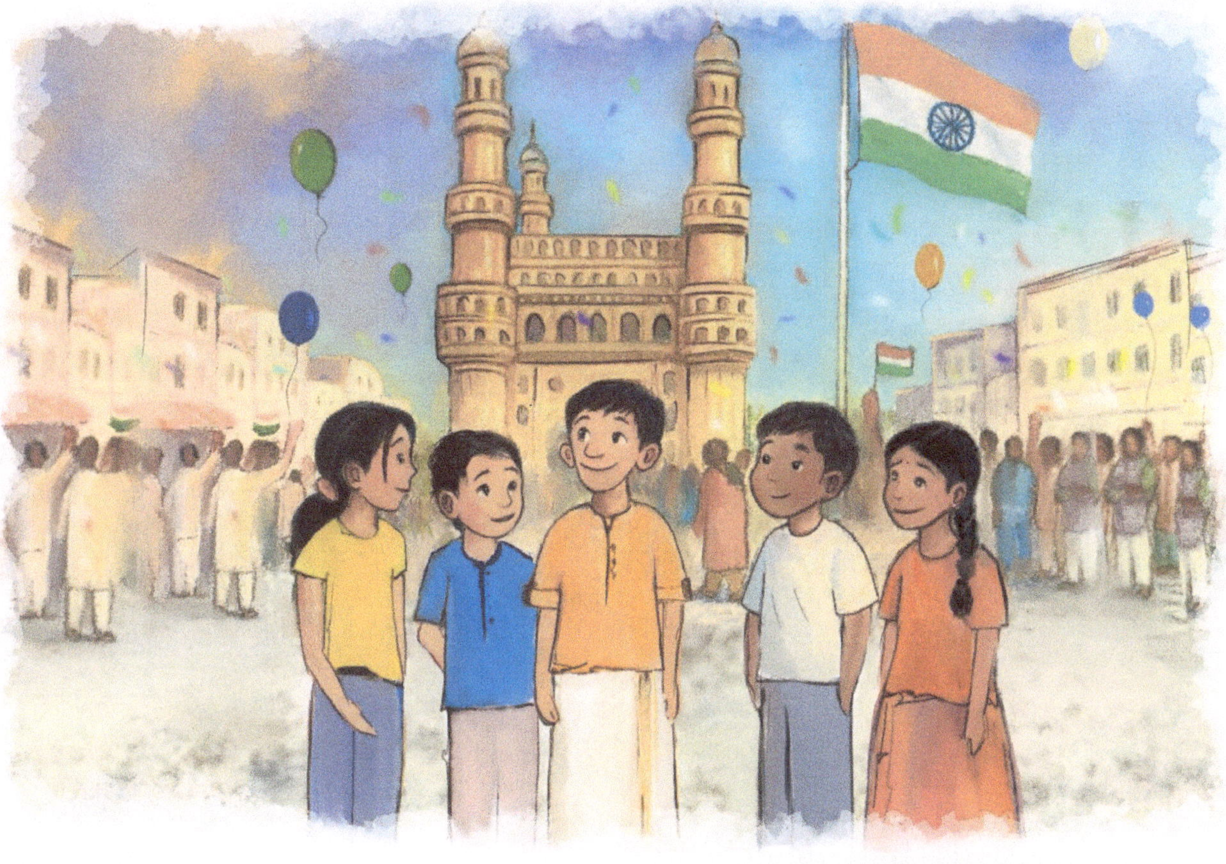

As the sounds of the anthem faded and the celebration slowly ended, the children noticed something troubling...

Tiny paper flags lay scattered on the ground—flags that had been waved only for a few moments, then carelessly thrown away. Crumpled, torn, and trampled, the flags lay forgotten on the dirt.
Dhruva bent down and gently picked one up, his brows furrowed.
"Why are we throwing these away?" he asked softly.

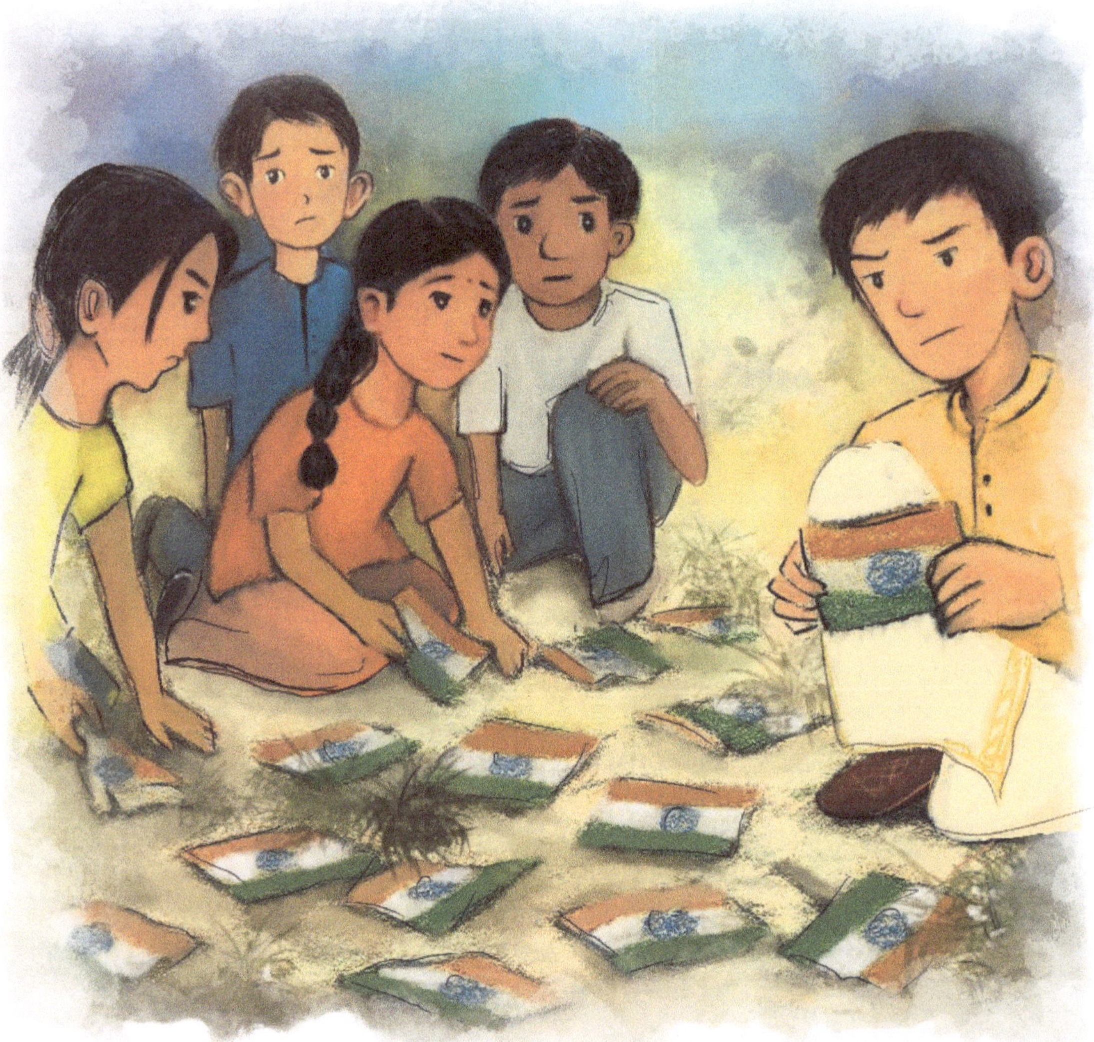

Parnika nodded, her voice thoughtful. "We just celebrated our freedom. This... doesn't feel right."
Shaurya looked around, puzzled. "Do people not know how important the flag is?"
Guhita stood tall. "Let's clean them up. This isn't how we treat our flag."

The children sat near the pile of discarded flags, gently folding each one with care. Vihaan, quiet but sincere, added, "We need to clean up and make sure that people understand how important the flag is. It represents our country, our freedom, and everything we stand for."

Then, something unexpected happened.

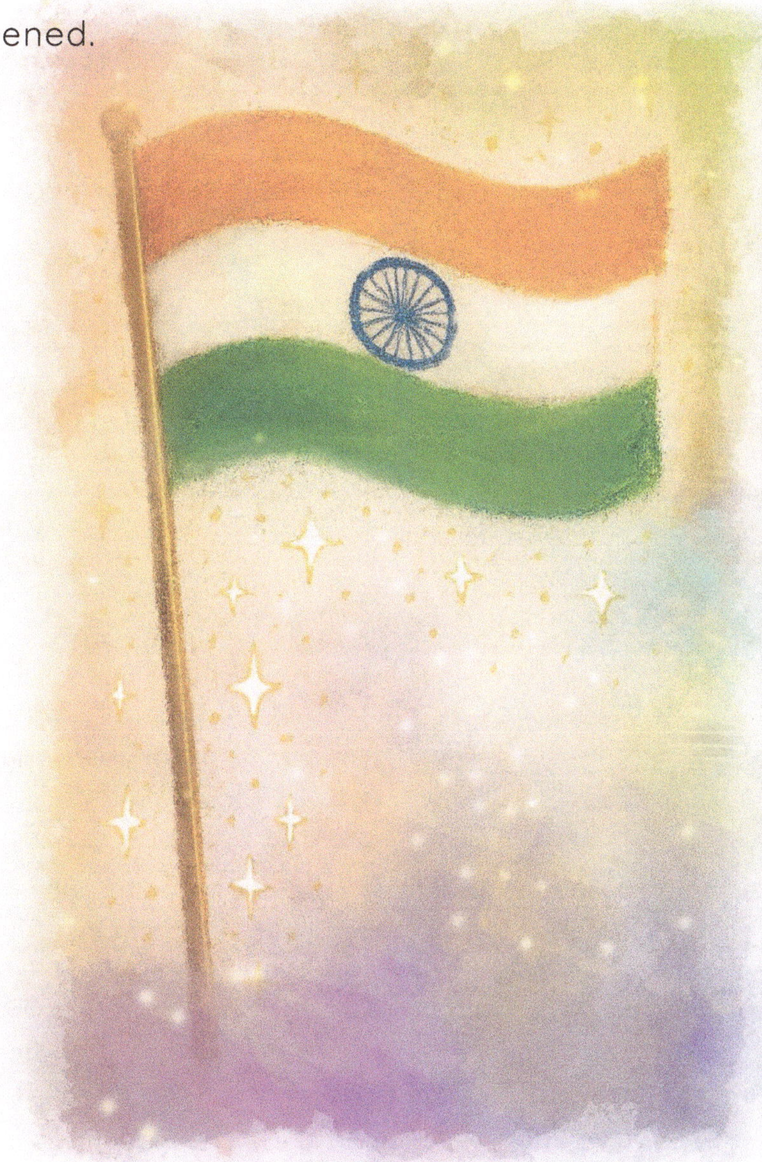

The children heard a soft whisper.

"Who's there?" asked Parnika, looking around.
"Is someone talking?" Dhruva whispered back, looking puzzled.

The flag fluttered in the breeze, and then they heard it again—a soft, almost sad voice.
"Who... who is picking me up?" the voice whispered.

Dhruva and his friends froze in surprise. They looked up at the flag standing tall, its fabric swaying gently in the wind.

The flag seemed to be moving, almost as if it was alive.

"Did... did the flag just speak?" Shaurya asked, his voice full of awe. Dhruva nodded, his eyes wide."It did! The flag is talking!"

The flag, now gazing down at the children, looked just as startled as they were.
"How... how can you hear me? No one has ever heard my voice before," it whispered, almost in disbelief.

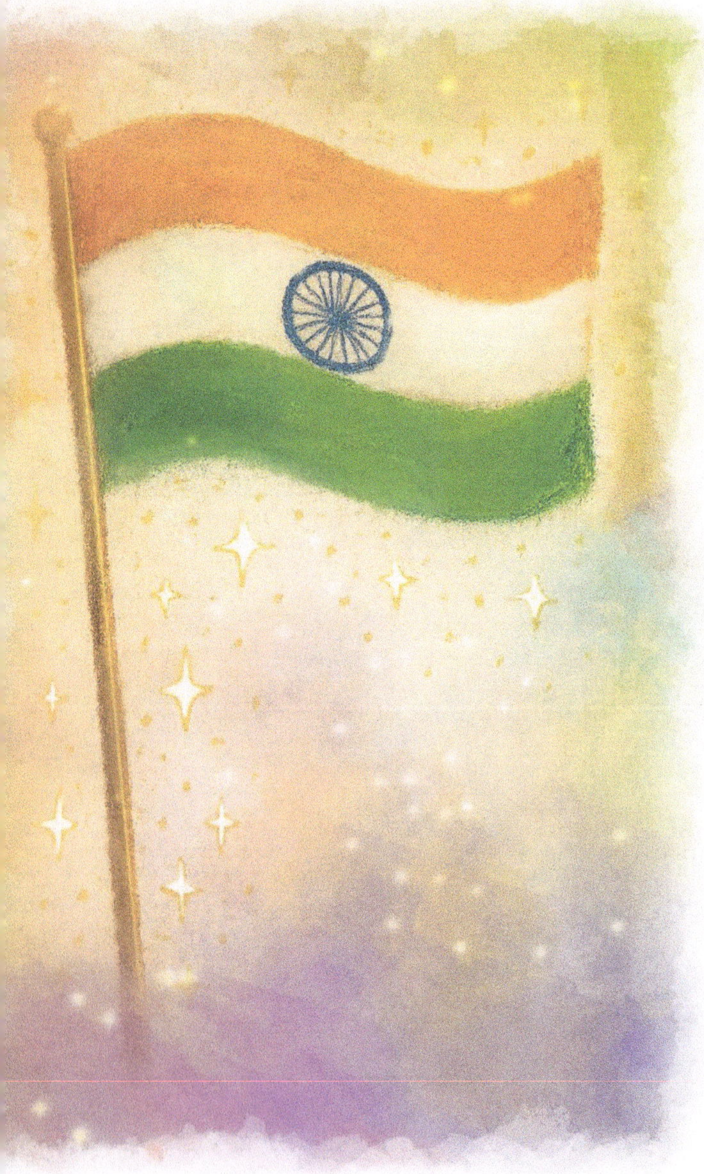

The children exchanged wide-eyed glances, their hearts racing with wonder. Slowly, they stepped closer, their curiosity overcoming their surprise.

"We can hear you," Dhruva said softly. "But... why do you sound so sad? Is something troubling you?"

Together, the children leaned in, their voices blending in a hopeful chorus. "Please... tell us what's on your mind."

The children's words seemed to linger in the air. For a moment, the flag was silent, its fabric rustling softly as though gathering the courage to speak. Then, with a gentle flutter in the wind, it began.

"I am not just any flag," it said. "I have been here for a long time, witnessing the rise of this great country, standing proudly during moments of triumph, and feeling the sorrow of being forgotten."

The flag's voice became softer but filled with power. "Come with me, children," it whispered. "Let me show you my journey through time. Let me tell you the stories of how I was born, how I grew, and how I came to represent the spirit of this land."

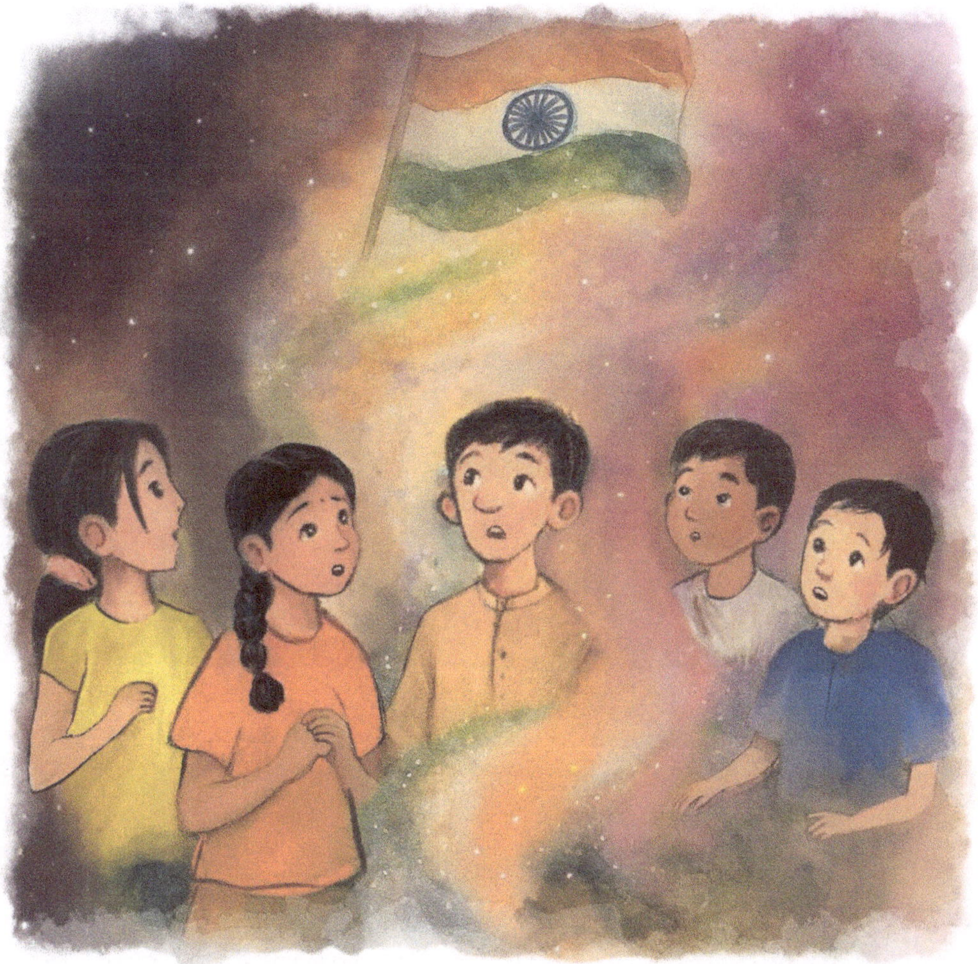

The moment they touched the flag, the world around them began to blur and spin. Dhruva held the flag tighter. Shaurya grabbed Guhita's hand. Parnika and Vihaan closed their eyes. The soft, glowing light grew brighter, and the next thing they knew, they were standing in a different time. With this the Flag turned into a time machine for the children.

When the swirling light settled, Dhruva and friends found themselves standing in a busy street, much older than they remembered. There were no cars or buildings like the City they knew. Instead, people were walking in long skirts, turbans, and traditional clothes, with carts selling spices and fruits.
"Where are we?" asked Parnika, looking around in awe. "This isn't Hyderabad! It looks like... like it's India, but it's so different!"

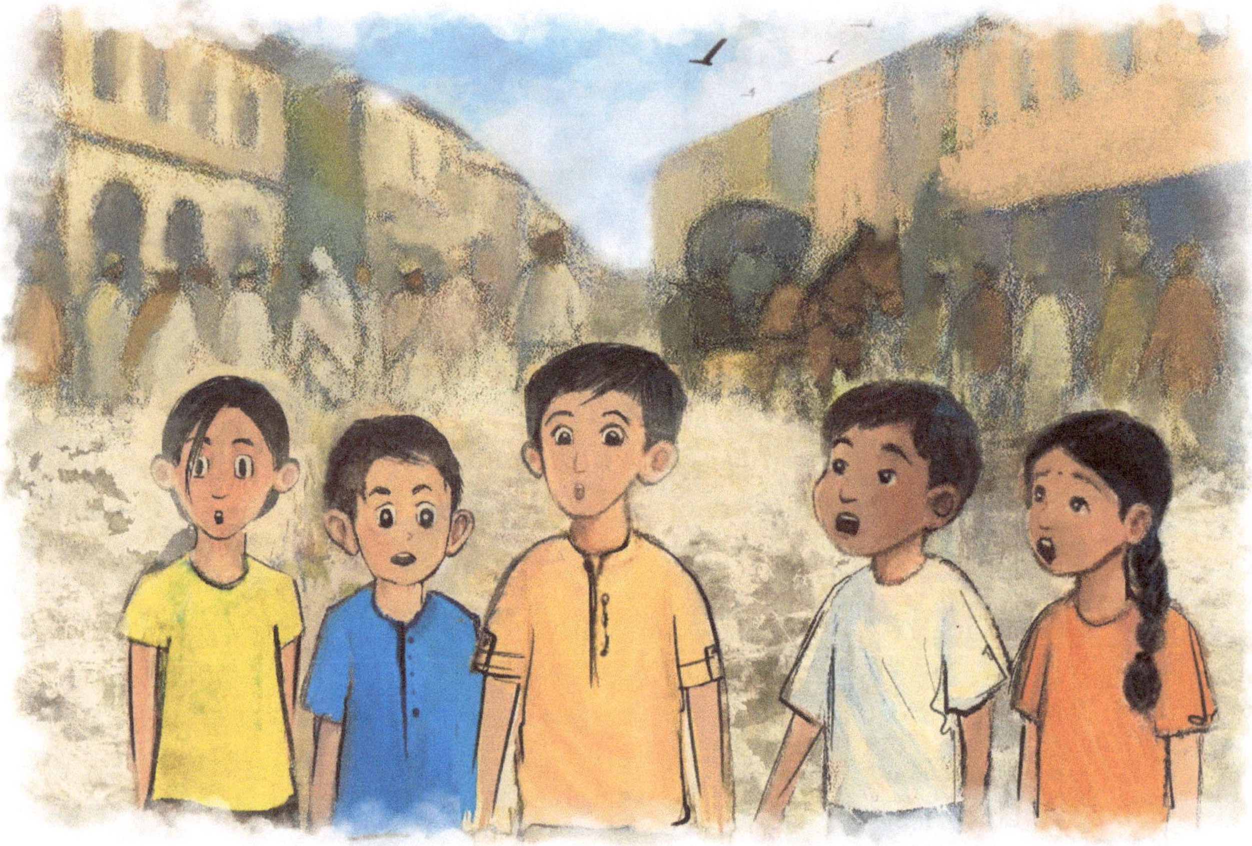

The flag, now glowing softly, fluttered in the breeze only visible to the kids, almost as if it was inviting them to follow. "You're in the early 1900s," it explained. "This is a time when India was still under British rule. The flag that you will see here is not yet the one you know today."

As the children held the flag tightly, they felt another swirl of energy. When the spinning stopped, the children found themselves standing in a room lit with bright lanterns and passionate voices.

A woman with kind eyes and a determined smile was painting something on fabric.
"Who is she?" whispered Vihaan.

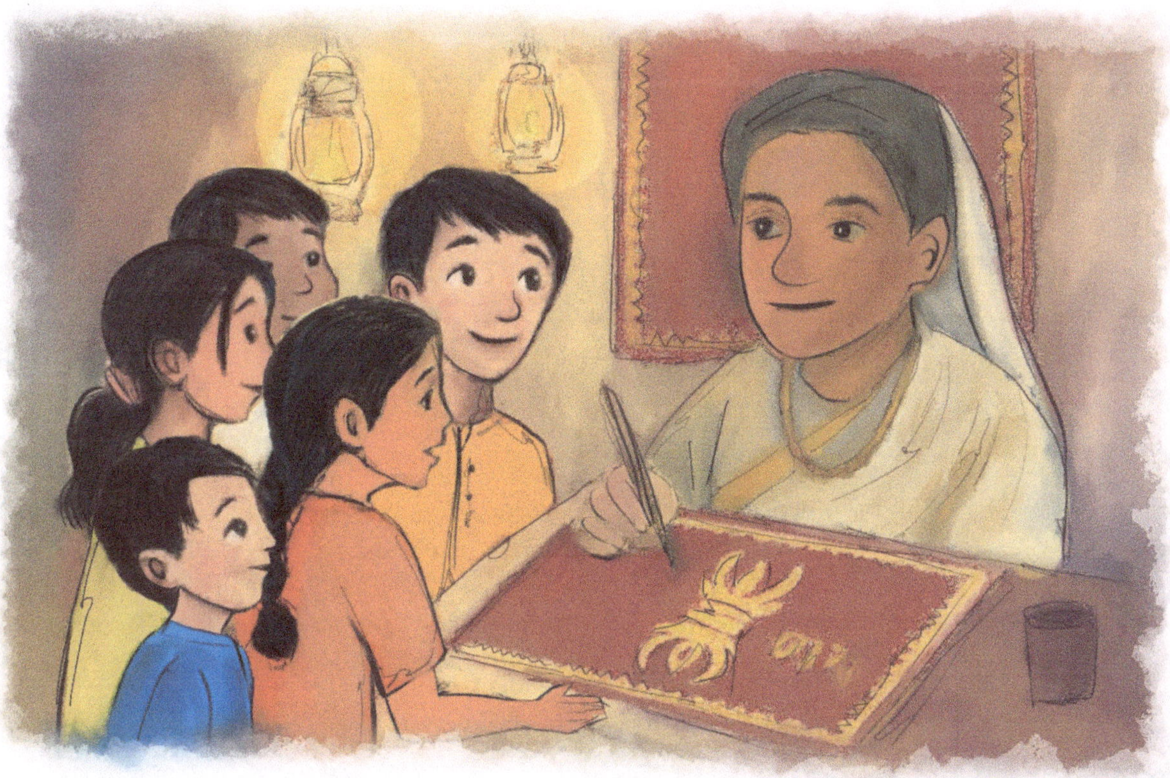

The flag whispered back, "That's Sister Nivedita. She was one of the first to design a flag for India—around 1905. She wasn't born here, but her heart belonged to this land. She was an Irish disciple of Swami Vivekananda." On the table was a flag—red and yellow with a bold symbol in the center.

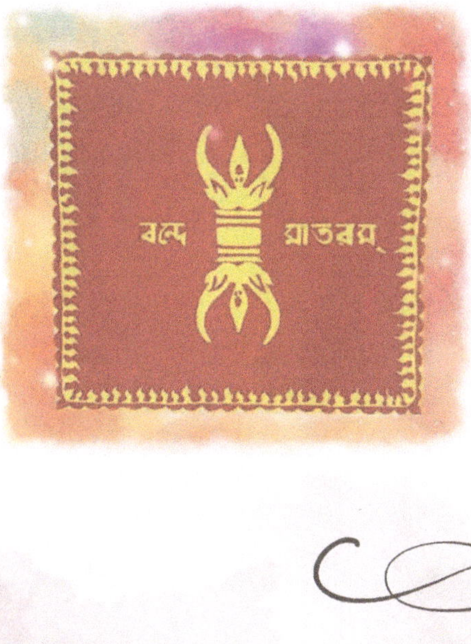

"That's the Vajra," explained the flag.
"It's the thunderbolt of Lord Indra, a symbol of strength. This flag represented India's spirit of courage and freedom, even before the world saw us as free."

Parnika admired the colours. "It's powerful... and simple."
Shaurya squinted. "But I've never seen this in our books."

"That's why I brought you here," said the flag. "To remember the forgotten stories."
In a blink, the light spun again—and they landed on a busy street in Paris, 1907.
Posters lined the walls. A crowd gathered around a woman holding a flag high above her head.

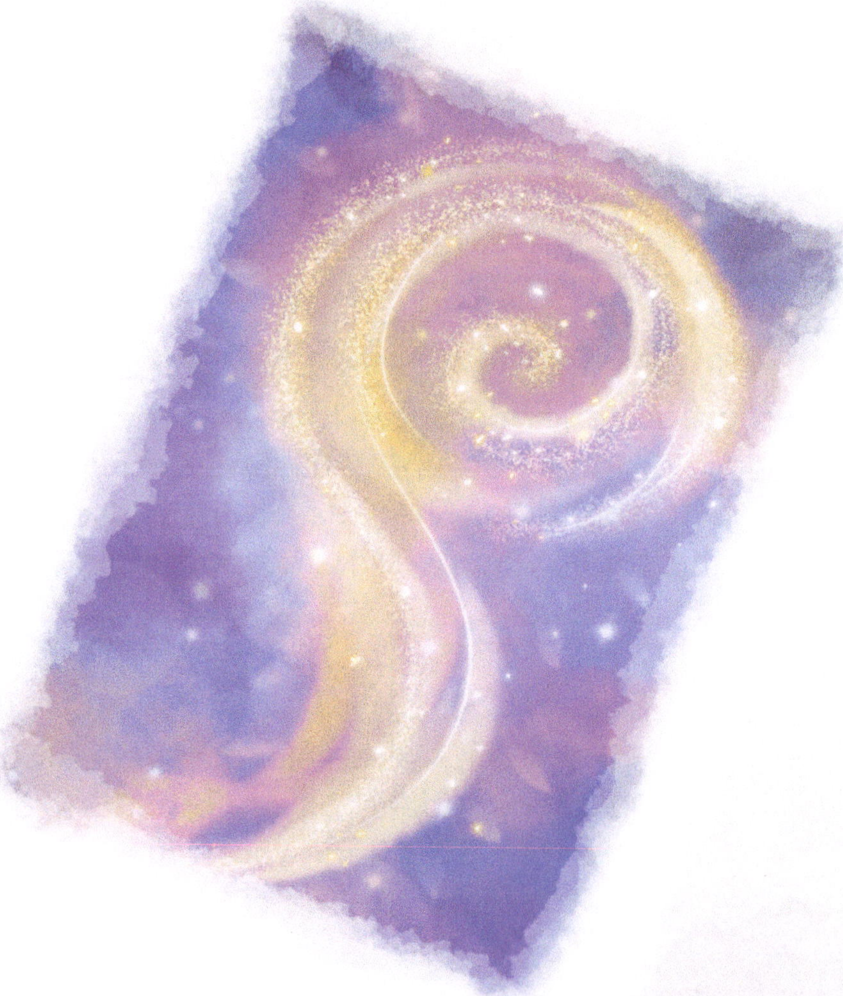

"That's Madame Bhikaiji Cama," the flag said proudly. "She raised this flag at a meeting of exiled revolutionaries. It was the first time the Indian flag was unfurled on foreign soil."

The flag shimmered—green on top, saffron in the middle, red at the bottom.
Eight lotus flowers bloomed on the green stripe. In the center, the words "Vande Mataram." And below, the sun and moon.

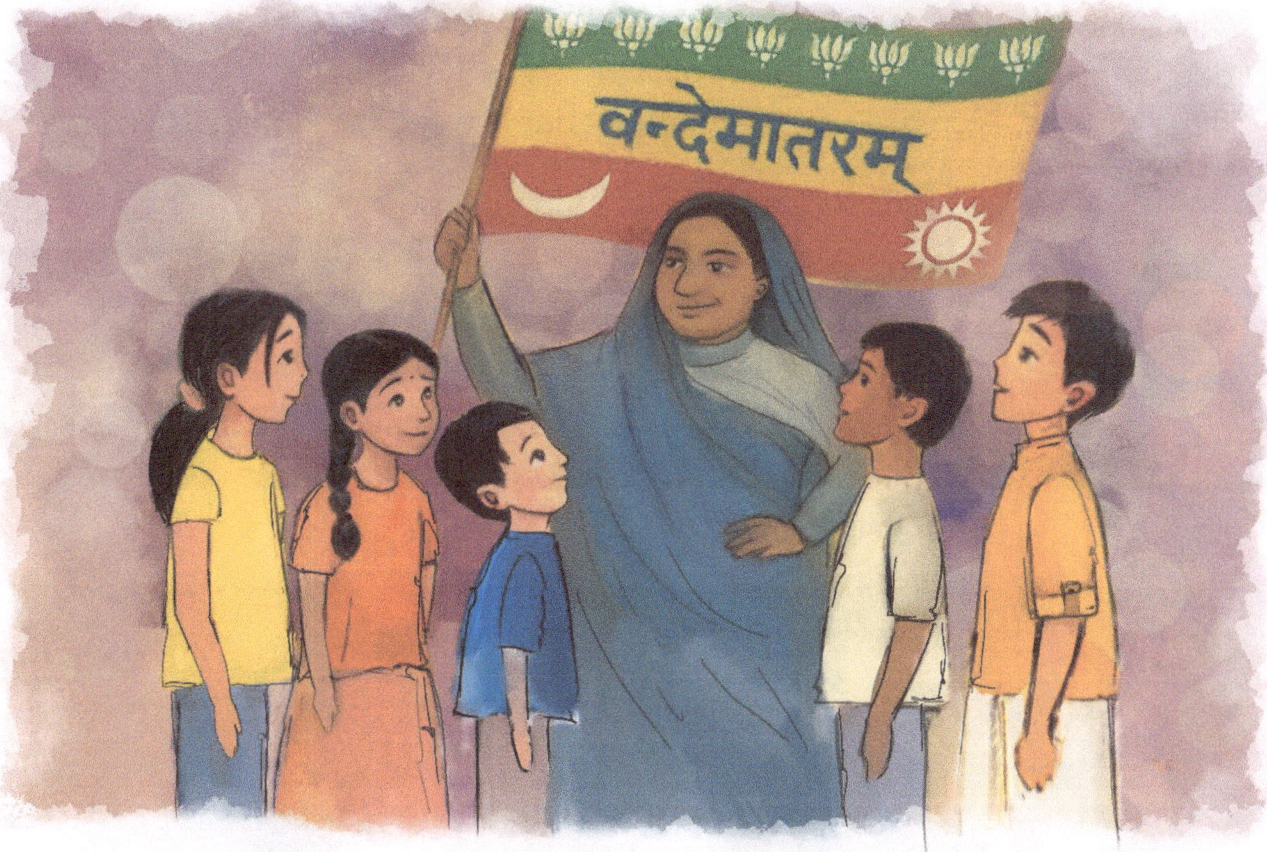

"She carried this flag when it wasn't safe to do so," the flag continued. "This was a shout to the world: India will rise."
Guhita beamed. "She was so brave."
Vihaan whispered, "And this flag... it's full of hope."

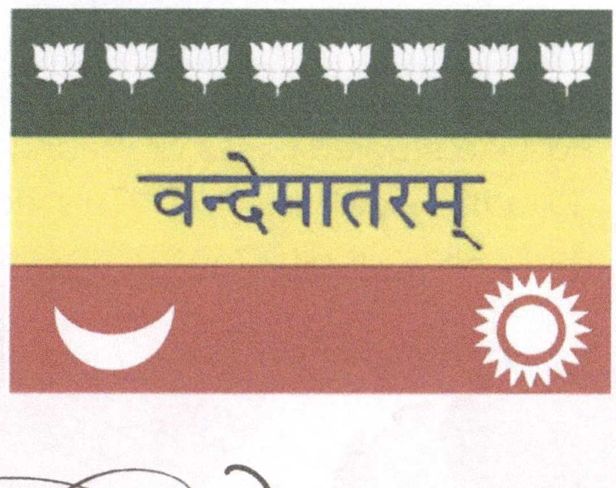

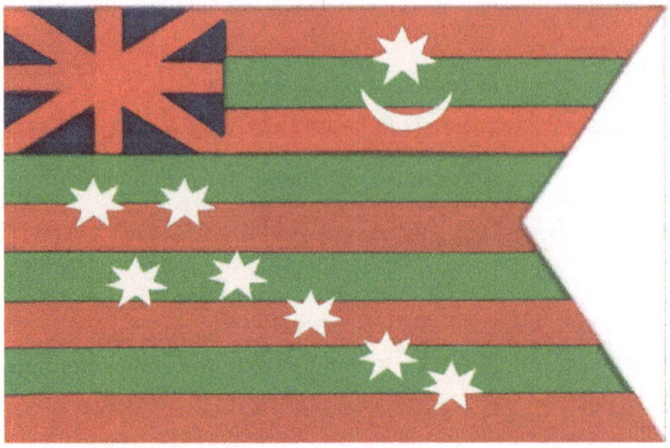

The air shimmered once more, and suddenly the children stood amidst a huge crowd.
People chanted slogans. Banners waved. A large flag fluttered in the breeze.

"Where are we now?" asked Shaurya.

"This is India, 1917," said the flag. "And that's Annie Besant, standing beside Lokmanya Tilak.
They led the Home Rule Movement—demanding self-governance for Indians."

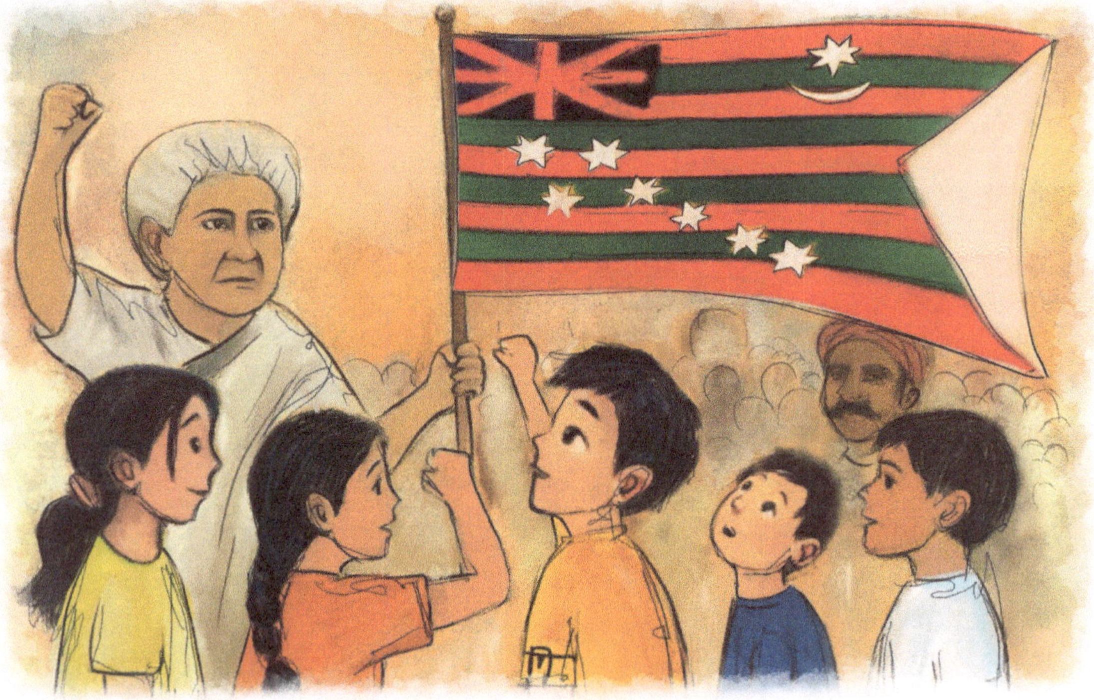

In the corner, the British Union Jack. Beside it, a white crescent moon and star, and in the center, seven stars forming the Saptarishi constellation.
Parnika studied it. "It's like many voices stitched together."
"Exactly," said the flag. "This flag spoke of unity—across religions, regions, and beliefs. It didn't last long, but it made a bold statement: India is ready to stand tall."
Guhita raised her fist. "And it wasn't just talk. It was a beginning."

As the fight for freedom grew more intense, so did I. I continued to grow and change and with that the wind returned, carrying them to a busy ground in Bezwada, 1921 (now Vijayawada).

A humble man with bright eyes and a kind smile stood in front of a cloth design.
"That's Pingali Venkayya," said the flag, its voice filled with pride. "He believed India needed her own identity—a flag for the people, not rulers."

The design was simple yet powerful—red and green stripes, representing different communities. Red represented the Hindus and other communities, while green symbolized Muslims.

Then Gandhiji arrived and suggested a change:
"Add a white stripe," he said. "To represent peace and unity among all religions... and a spinning wheel—the Charkha—for self-reliance."

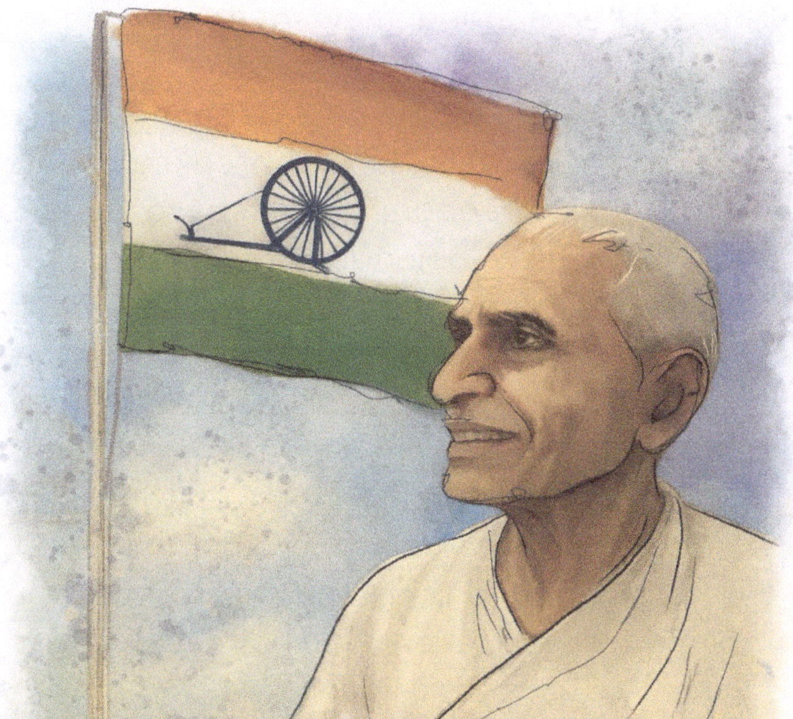

At that time, Gandhi was encouraging Indians to spin their own cloth using the Charkha as a way to boycott British goods.

So, the spinning wheel in the flag became a powerful symbol of independence and self-sufficiency.

The children saw the Charkha spin, right at the center.

"Why do you have this wheel in the middle?" Dhruva asked softly, pointing at the deep blue circle. "Wasn't there once a charkha here?"

The Flag sighed softly, as if remembering a long journey.
"For years, I carried the Charkha with pride," it said. "Through struggle, marches, and sacrifice. Through it, Gandhiji taught our people to spin their own cloth, to depend on their own strength, to say no to foreign rule. The charkha made me a symbol of courage and swadeshi."

The children nodded, their faces glowing with respect.

"But then," the Flag's voice deepened, "a time came when the chains of British rule were finally breaking. A new India was about to be born. And my leaders asked me a question: Should I still carry the charkha, which belonged to one movement? Or should I carry something that belongs to every Indian, for all time?"

The Flag swayed, the blue wheel at its heart catching the sunlight.
"That is when they chose the Ashoka Chakra — the eternal wheel of dharma, taken from the Lion Capital at Sarnath. Unlike the charkha, it was not just about cloth, or one movement. It was about the law of truth, justice, and progress. Its twenty-four spokes remind us to keep moving forward, every hour of every day."

Parnika whispered, "So the charkha was like the fight for freedom... and the chakra is for everything India will become?"
The Flag fluttered proudly.
"Yes, dear children. The charkha carried us to freedom. The chakra carries us into the future."

The Flag's voice softened, almost like it was turning the page of time.

The light around the children shimmered once more—this time glowing warmer, brighter.

Now the children were standing in a quiet, majestic hall with people in white khadi and thoughtful faces.

"This is the Constituent Assembly of India in July 1947," the flag whispered.

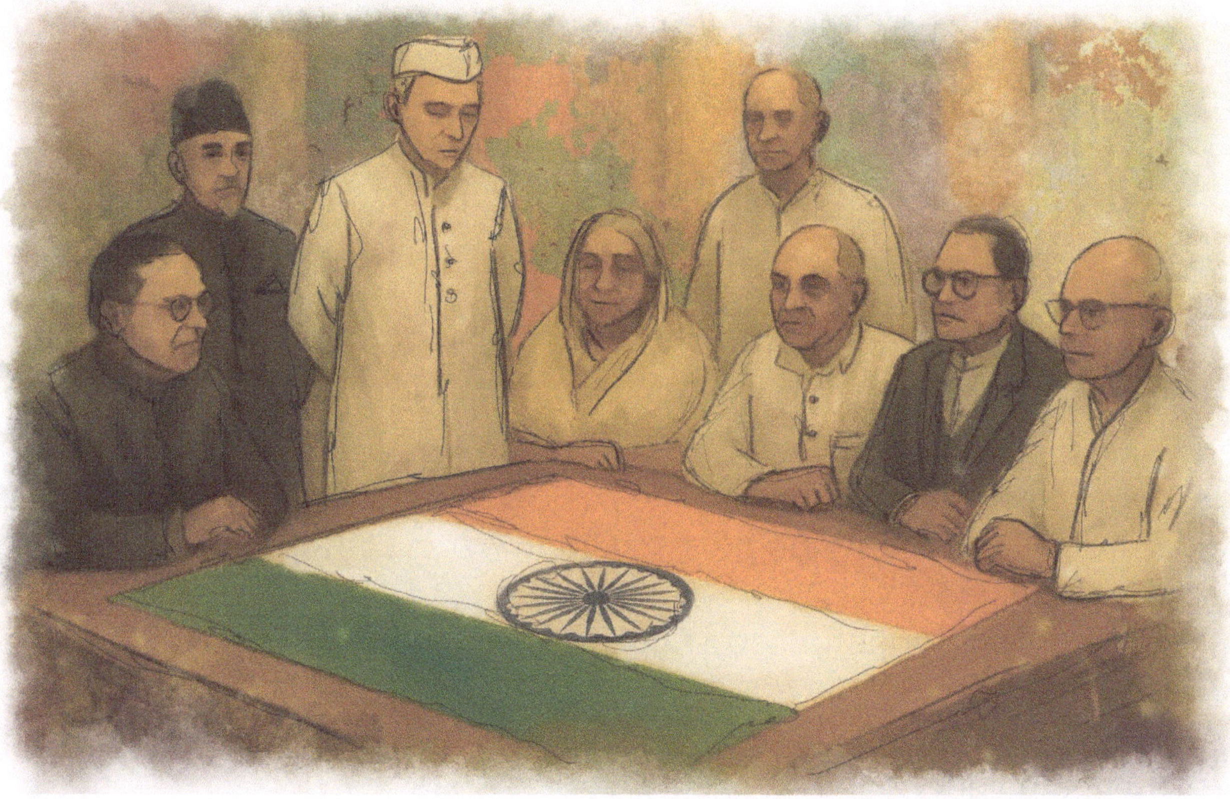

"Here, India's leaders came together to decide the final version of our national flag."

In the center lay the cloth—saffron, white, and green. And at its heart, glowing proudly, was the navy blue Ashoka Chakra.
Shaurya gasped. "That's it! That's our flag!"

The Flag fluttered proudly. “Yes. At last, the tricolor had found its true form. A flag not just of struggle, but of a free nation ready to walk into the future.”

The flag’s voice turned soft, almost like a lullaby.
“That’s Dr. Rajendra Prasad,” it said, pointing to a tall, kind-eyed man.
“He’s about to declare me as the official flag of free India.”

The children watched as Dr. Prasad rose before the Assembly and said with quiet strength: “This flag shall be our National Flag—a symbol of freedom, unity, and the values we hold dear.”

The room erupted in applause.

“Look!” said Guhita, pointing. “That’s Chacha Nehru!”
“Yes,” said the flag. “He became India’s first Prime Minister—and one of the strongest voices for my adoption.”

“There’s Sarojini Naidu, the Nightingale of India,” said Vihaan, eyes sparkling.

“And Sardar Patel, Dr. Ambedkar, Maulana Azad, C. Rajagopalachari...” the flag continued.
“All of them stood together to shape not just this flag, but the India it represents.”

Just then, the light changed once more.
The children were standing outside the Red Fort, on the morning of August 15, 1947.

A sea of people gathered as Pandit Nehru stepped forward and raised the new flag high above the crowd.
“Vande Mataram! Bharat Mata Ki Jai!” rang through the air.

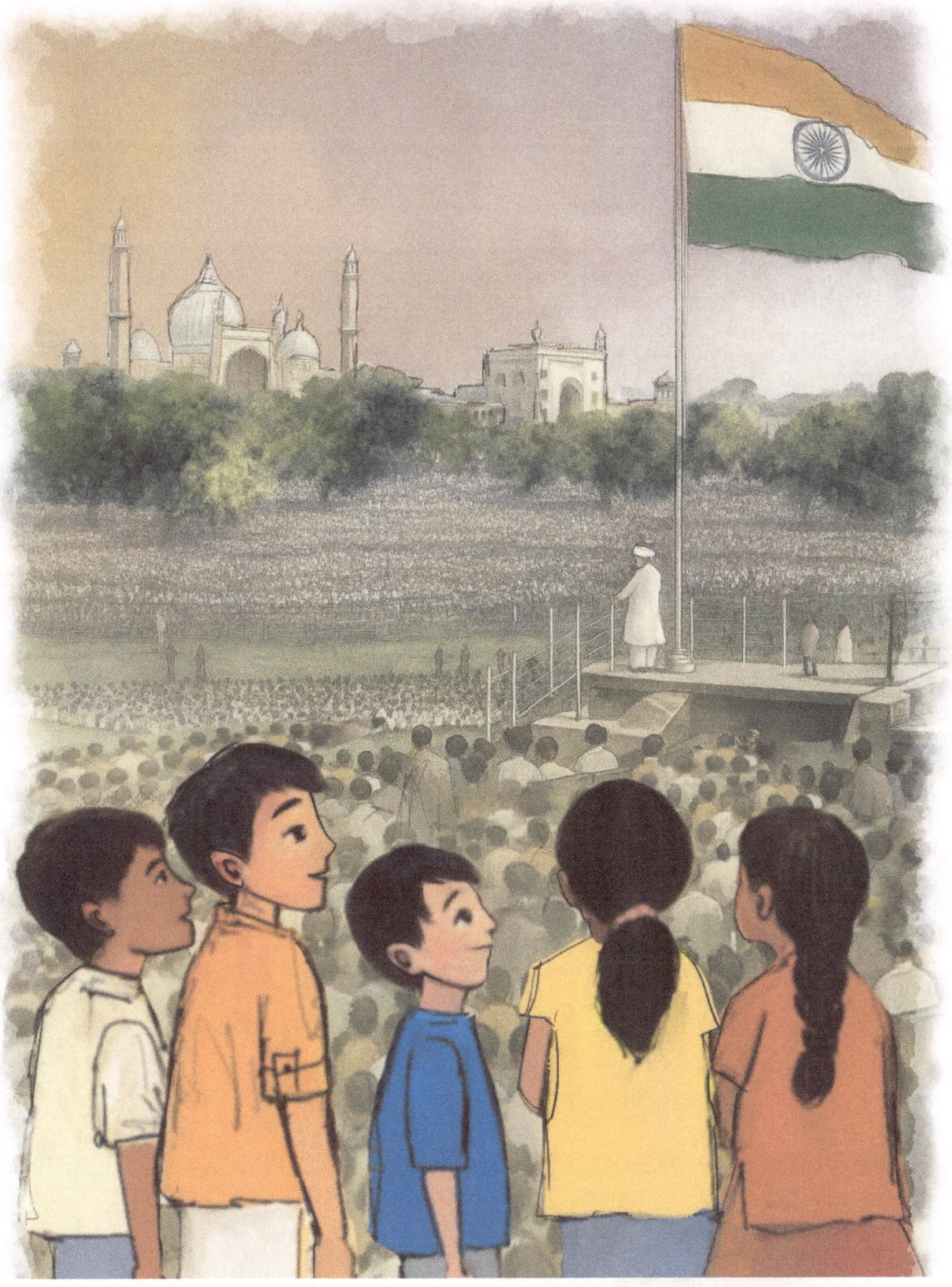

Parnika smiled thoughtfully. “I'll never see the flag the same way again. You're more than just colours and stripes.
It's sad how we met you—a symbol of our Nation's pride shouldn't be left to landfill.”

Dhruva nodded.
“You've taught us so much about your history.
Surely, the people who made you our Nation's symbol had rules to protect your honor.
Can you tell us about them? We should know how to preserve your glory.”

The flag fluttered gently, its voice calm and steady.

“Yes, there are rules called **“The Flag code of India”**—meant not just to protect me, but to remind every Indian of what I stand for. Let me tell you about them.”

"The Flag Code"

How to Respect Our Flag

Proper Display of the Flag

- The saffron band must always be at the top when hoisting the flag; displaying it upside down indicates distress and is disrespectful.
- The flag should always be given a position of prominence and displayed with dignity, ensuring it is placed above all other flags.
- When displayed alongside other flags, the Indian flag must be positioned either at the highest point or to the extreme left.

Timing and Occasions for Hoisting

- The flag should be hoisted only between sunrise and sunset, irrespective of the weather.
- It can be displayed on public and national holidays, special occasions, and important events.
- Citizens are encouraged to hoist the flag at their homes or premises on such occasions.

Handling of the Flag

- The flag must always be kept off the ground, water, or any unclean surface.
- It should be handled with utmost care and folded properly when not in use.
- The flag must not be used as a covering for tables, vehicles, or podiums.

Prohibited Uses

- The flag must not be used as a decoration, drapery, or incorporated into costumes.
- It should never be printed on items such as cushions, handkerchiefs, clothing, or other daily-use objects.
- The flag is prohibited from being used for commercial activities, advertisements, or the promotion of any business or product.

How to Respect Our Flag

Respectful Conduct During Hoisting:

- All individuals present must stand at attention to show respect when the flag is being hoisted or lowered.
- Citizens are required to salute the flag during its hoisting or lowering.
- The flag must remain intact and unaltered throughout the ceremony.

Disposal of the Flag:

- If the flag is torn, damaged, or no longer suitable for display, it should be disposed of respectfully and with dignity, ideally by burning it in private.
- The flag should never be discarded casually or thrown away.

Hoisting by Citizens:

- The Flag Code of India allows citizens to hoist the flag on private property, as long as all the rules of the code are followed.
- Citizens are encouraged to display the flag during national celebrations to promote patriotism and unity.

Legal Protections for the Flag:

The Prevention of Insults to National Honour Act, 1971, safeguards the Indian flag from any form of insult or disrespect. Violating the Flag Code or engaging in acts of disrespect towards the flag is punishable under the law.

Dhruva looked down, voice quiet.
"We know flags shouldn't be thrown on the ground. That's why we came back to clean up.
But... we didn't know there were actual rules to protect you."

The flag fluttered gently, its voice kind.
"Don't be too hard on yourselves. Many don't know the Flag Code of India.
It's not always taught—but that's why I'm here. So you can carry this knowledge forward."

Parnika sighed. "It's such a shame. You stand for everything we believe in—freedom, unity, pride. Why aren't we taught this in school or at home?"

Shaurya's fists clenched. "It's not just about rules. It's about respect.
You carry the dreams of a nation, and we've forgotten how to honor that."

The flag rippled softly, as if comforting them.
"But now you know. And that changes everything.
Start by showing your love through small actions. Teach others. Let your respect become a ripple."

As the flag's voice faded, the children found themselves once more near the Charminar.
The sounds of the Independence Day celebration returned—but something had changed.

The air felt different... heavier with meaning.

The children knelt down and began picking up the fallen flags—slowly, gently, respectfully.
At first, only a few people noticed. Some watched, confused. Then—a couple of teenagers joined in. An elderly woman straightened a crumpled flag with care.

More and more people gathered, silently moved by the children's quiet act.
Soon, a crowd had formed.
What began with five kids became a movement.
Vihaan looked around, wide-eyed. "Are they all... helping because of us?"

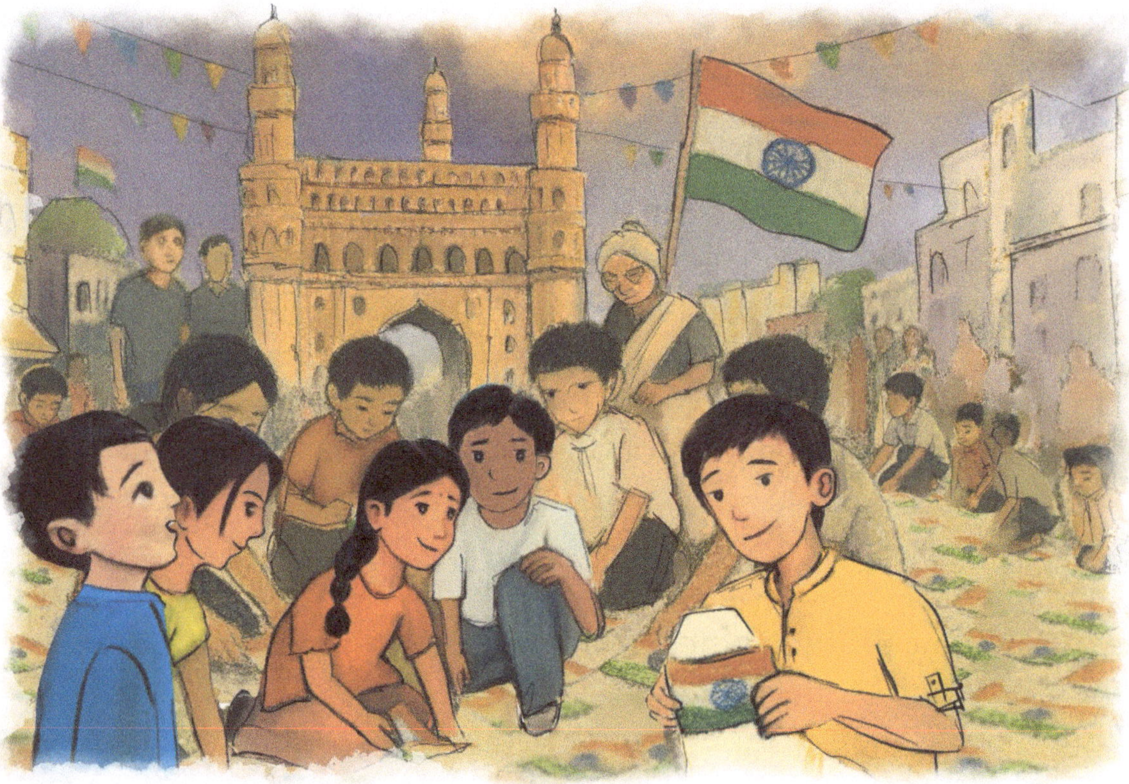

Dhruva smiled. "Maybe this is how change begins.
It starts small—but when you care, others do too."
Guhita nodded. "It's not just about cleaning up.
It's about showing we still believe in what the flag stands for."

When the cleanup was done, the Charminar stood tall once again surrounded by a cleaner space... and a renewed respect. The children turned to leave, tired but proud. As they glanced back, the flag fluttered in the breeze, and for a moment, it almost seemed to wink at them.

Then came a whisper... one only they could hear: "Whenever you see me flying, remember I carry the stories of those who fought and dreamed for freedom.
I belong to all of you, and I couldn't be more proud."

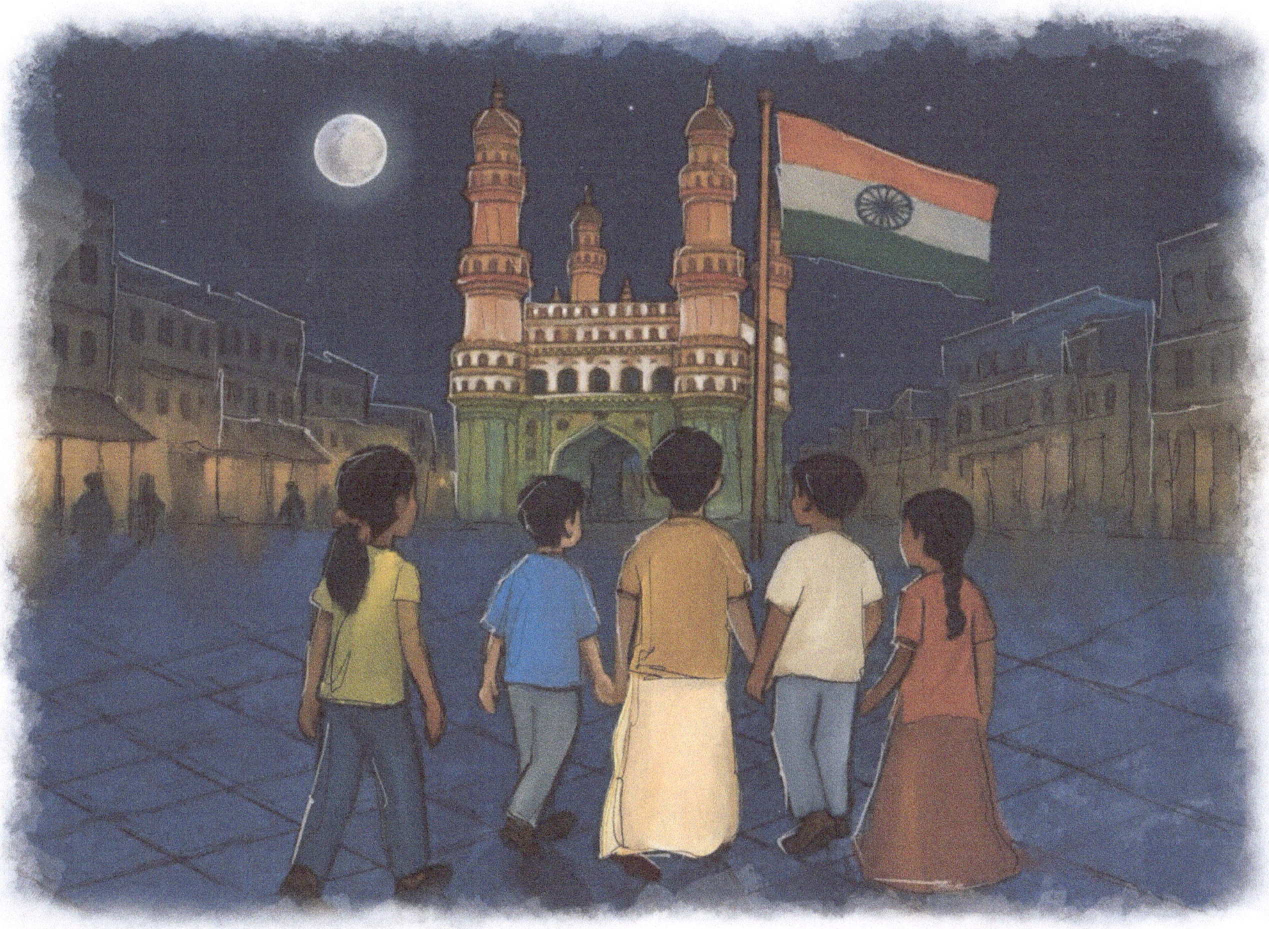

JAI HIND

THE END

Reflection & Engagement Prompts

My Flag, My Heart: Can you draw how you feel when you see the flag flying high?

What does the flag mean to you? What would you say if it could hear you?

My Promise to the Flag (You can write or Draw)

"I promise to respect the Indian Flag by..."

Whisper to the Reader

· A final message from the flag to the reader:

"I may not have a voice, but through your respect, I speak.
Whenever you see me fly, remember the stories I carry,
and let your actions tell the world how proud you are to be part of this nation."
"You are now a Whisper Keeper—thank you for listening."

About the Author

Sweta Sanapala is a passionate storyteller, mother, and lifelong learner. Inspired by her childhood memories of Independence Day and the magic in her son's questions, she wrote The Flag's Whisper to help children fall in love with the Indian flag all over again.

She believes that stories have the power to awaken pride, empathy, and action—and hopes this one does the same for you.

The idea for this book was sparked by a visit to a doctor's clinic with her son. There, she spotted a wooden India map puzzle that included five earlier designs of the Indian flag. Intrigued, she encouraged her son to replicate them through drawing. Seeing the evolution of the flag in such a visual way deeply moved her.

When she later shared her son's artwork with friends, many expressed surprise—they had no idea the Indian flag had gone through so many changes. That moment became a realization: more people, especially children, should be made aware of this hidden chapter of our heritage.

And what better way to share it than through a heartfelt story?

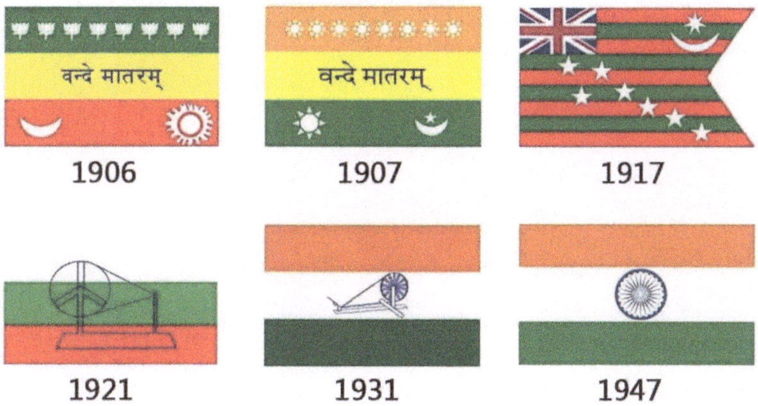

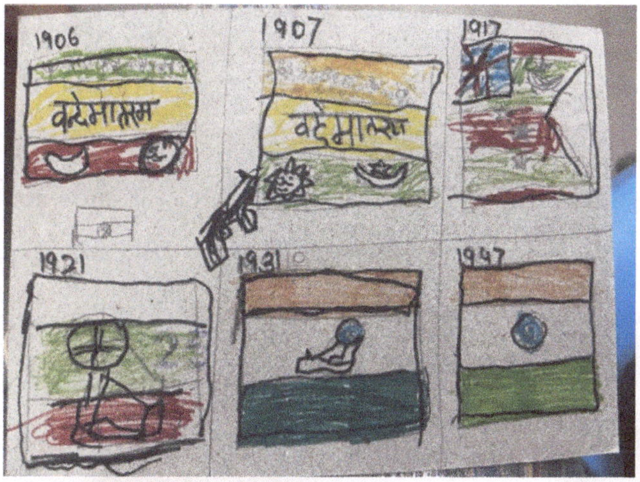

🌟 Stay Connected

If this story touched your heart or sparked curiosity in your child, I'd love to hear from you!

📬 Email: littleindiabooks@gmail.com
📸 Instagram: @littleindiabooks

✏️ Inspired by the Flag?
Children love drawing what moves them—just like my son did. If your little reader created their own version of the Indian flag or wrote a message to the flag, I'd be honored to see it!

🎨 Share your child's artwork or writing:
Tag me on Instagram with #TheFlagsWhisper
or
email it to littleindiabooks@gmail.com

Selected entries will be featured in our stories and get discount on our future books